Gratitude Journal for kids

D1055990

THIS BOOK BELONGS TO...

_____

_____

_____

ALL ABOUT ME

MY NAME IS

_ _ _ _ _ _ _ _ _ _ _

this is me

I am ( ) years old

My birthday is

My favorite:

animal _ _ _ _ _ _ _ _ _ _

book _ _ _ _ _ _ _ _ _ _

color _ _ _ _ _ _ _ _ _ _

sport _ _ _ _ _ _ _ _ _ _

food _ _ _ _ _ _ _ _ _ _

I live in

My family

When I grow up I want to be

Date [   ]

Today I'm thankful for:

1 [   ]

2 [   ]

3 [   ]

How I feel today:

HAPPY   EXCITED   TIRED   SAD
○   ○   ○   ○

SURPRISED   MAD   LONELY   SILLY
○   ○   ○   ○

Something wonderful will happen tomorrow:

1 _____

2 _____

3 _____

Date [_____]

Today I'm thankful for:

1 [_____]

2 [_____]

3 [_____]

How I feel today:

HAPPY	EXCITED	TIRED	SAD
◯	◯	◯	◯

SURPRISED	MAD	LONELY	SILLY
◯	◯	◯	◯

Something wonderful will happen tomorrow:

1 _____

2 _____

3 _____

Date [   ]

Today I'm thankful for:

1 [   ]

2 [   ]

3 [   ]

How I feel today:

HAPPY	EXCITED	TIRED	SAD
◯	◯	◯	◯

SURPRISED	MAD	LONELY	SILLY
◯	◯	◯	◯

Something wonderful will happen tomorrow:

1 _____

2 _____

3 _____

Date ⬭

Today I'm thankful for:

1 ⬭

2 ⬭

3 ⬭

How I feel today:

HAPPY	EXCITED	TIRED	SAD
◯	◯	◯	◯

SURPRISED	MAD	LONELY	SILLY
◯	◯	◯	◯

Something wonderful will happen tomorrow:

1 _____

2 _____

3 _____

Date [   ]

Today I'm thankful for:

1 [   ]

2 [   ]

3 [   ]

How I feel today:

HAPPY   EXCITED   TIRED   SAD

◯   ◯   ◯   ◯

SURPRISED   MAD   LONELY   SILLY

◯   ◯   ◯   ◯

Something wonderful will happen tomorrow:

1 _____

2 _____

3 _____

Date [ ]

Today I'm thankful for:

1 [ ]

2 [ ]

3 [ ]

How I feel today:

HAPPY   EXCITED   TIRED   SAD
◯   ◯   ◯   ◯

SURPRISED   MAD   LONELY   SILLY
◯   ◯   ◯   ◯

Something wonderful will happen tomorrow:

1 _____

2 _____

3 _____

Date

Today I'm thankful for:

1.
2.
3.

How I feel today:

HAPPY	EXCITED	TIRED	SAD
○	○	○	○

SURPRISED	MAD	LONELY	SILLY
○	○	○	○

Something wonderful will happen tomorrow:

1 _____

2 _____

3 _____

The best things that happened to me

_____

_____

_____

_____

People I'm thankful for

_____

_____

_____

_____

I learned

_____

_____

_____

_____

Date [_____]

Today I'm thankful for:

1 [_____]

2 [_____]

3 [_____]

How I feel today:

HAPPY   EXCITED   TIRED   SAD
○   ○   ○   ○

SURPRISED   MAD   LONELY   SILLY
○   ○   ○   ○

Something wonderful will happen tomorrow:

1 _____

2 _____

3 _____

Date

Today I'm thankful for:

1

2

3

How I feel today:

HAPPY   EXCITED   TIRED   SAD

○   ○   ○   ○

SURPRISED   MAD   LONELY   SILLY

○   ○   ○   ○

Something wonderful will happen tomorrow:

1 _____

2 _____

3 _____

Date [＿＿＿＿＿]

Today I'm thankful for:

1 [＿＿＿＿＿＿＿＿＿＿＿＿＿＿＿＿＿]

2 [＿＿＿＿＿＿＿＿＿＿＿＿＿＿＿＿＿]

3 [＿＿＿＿＿＿＿＿＿＿＿＿＿＿＿＿＿]

How I feel today:

HAPPY	EXCITED	TIRED	SAD
◯	◯	◯	◯

SURPRISED	MAD	LONELY	SILLY
◯	◯	◯	◯

Something wonderful will happen tomorrow:

1 ＿＿＿＿＿＿＿＿＿＿＿＿＿＿＿＿＿＿＿＿

2 ＿＿＿＿＿＿＿＿＿＿＿＿＿＿＿＿＿＿＿＿

3 ＿＿＿＿＿＿＿＿＿＿＿＿＿＿＿＿＿＿＿＿

Date _____

Today I'm thankful for:

1 _____

2 _____

3 _____

How I feel today:

HAPPY	EXCITED	TIRED	SAD
◯	◯	◯	◯

SURPRISED	MAD	LONELY	SILLY
◯	◯	◯	◯

Something wonderful will happen tomorrow:

1 _____

2 _____

3 _____

Date

Today I'm thankful for:

1
2
3

How I feel today:

HAPPY   EXCITED   TIRED   SAD

( )   ( )   ( )   ( )

SURPRISED   MAD   LONELY   SILLY

( )   ( )   ( )   ( )

Something wonderful will happen tomorrow:

1 _____

2 _____

3 _____

Date

Today I'm thankful for:

1
2
3

How I feel today:

HAPPY	EXCITED	TIRED	SAD
◯	◯	◯	◯

SURPRISED	MAD	LONELY	SILLY
◯	◯	◯	◯

Something wonderful will happen tomorrow:

1 _____

2 _____

3 _____

Date

Today I'm thankful for:

1
2
3

How I feel today:

HAPPY   EXCITED   TIRED   SAD

◯   ◯   ◯   ◯

SURPRISED   MAD   LONELY   SILLY

◯   ◯   ◯   ◯

Something wonderful will happen tomorrow:

1 _____

2 _____

3 _____

Follow your dreams

I have a dream _____
_____
_____
_____

I have a dream _____
_____
_____
_____

I have a dream _____
_____
_____
_____

Date ⬡

Today I'm thankful for:

1 _____

2 _____

3 _____

How I feel today:

HAPPY	EXCITED	TIRED	SAD
◯	◯	◯	◯

SURPRISED	MAD	LONELY	SILLY
◯	◯	◯	◯

Something wonderful will happen tomorrow:

1 _____

2 _____

3 _____

Date

Today I'm thankful for:

1

2

3

How I feel today:

HAPPY	EXCITED	TIRED	SAD
◯	◯	◯	◯
SURPRISED	MAD	LONELY	SILLY
◯	◯	◯	◯

Something wonderful will happen tomorrow:

1 _____

2 _____

3 _____

Date [_____]

Today I'm thankful for:

1 [_____]

2 [_____]

3 [_____]

How I feel today:

HAPPY   EXCITED   TIRED   SAD
( )   ( )   ( )   ( )

SURPRISED   MAD   LONELY   SILLY
( )   ( )   ( )   ( )

Something wonderful will happen tomorrow:

1 _____

2 _____

3 _____

Date ⬭

Today I'm thankful for:

1 ⬭

2 ⬭

3 ⬭

How I feel today:

HAPPY   EXCITED   TIRED   SAD

◯   ◯   ◯   ◯

SURPRISED   MAD   LONELY   SILLY

◯   ◯   ◯   ◯

Something wonderful will happen tomorrow:

1 _____

2 _____

3 _____

Date [   ]

Today I'm thankful for:

1 [   ]

2 [   ]

3 [   ]

How I feel today:

HAPPY	EXCITED	TIRED	SAD
○	○	○	○

SURPRISED	MAD	LONELY	SILLY
○	○	○	○

Something wonderful will happen tomorrow:

1 _____

2 _____

3 _____

Date

Today I'm thankful for:

1
2
3

How I feel today:

HAPPY   EXCITED   TIRED   SAD

◯   ◯   ◯   ◯

SURPRISED   MAD   LONELY   SILLY

◯   ◯   ◯   ◯

Something wonderful will happen tomorrow:

1 _____

2 _____

3 _____

Date ⬡

Today I'm thankful for:

1 ▭

2 ▭

3 ▭

How I feel today:

HAPPY	EXCITED	TIRED	SAD
◯	◯	◯	◯

SURPRISED	MAD	LONELY	SILLY
◯	◯	◯	◯

Something wonderful will happen tomorrow:

1 _____

2 _____

3 _____

DRAW YOUR DREAM

If you can dream it, You can do it!
- Walt Disney

Date [   ]

Today I'm thankful for:

1 [   ]

2 [   ]

3 [   ]

How I feel today:

| HAPPY | EXCITED | TIRED | SAD |
| ○ | ○ | ○ | ○ |

| SURPRISED | MAD | LONELY | SILLY |
| ○ | ○ | ○ | ○ |

Something wonderful will happen tomorrow:

1 _____

2 _____

3 _____

Date

Today I'm thankful for:

1 _____

2 _____

3 _____

How I feel today:

HAPPY ○   EXCITED ○   TIRED ○   SAD ○

SURPRISED ○   MAD ○   LONELY ○   SILLY ○

Something wonderful will happen tomorrow:

1 _____

2 _____

3 _____

Date

Today I'm thankful for:

1
2
3

How I feel today:

HAPPY   EXCITED   TIRED   SAD

◯   ◯   ◯   ◯

SURPRISED   MAD   LONELY   SILLY

◯   ◯   ◯   ◯

Something wonderful will happen tomorrow:

1 _____

2 _____

3 _____

Date [   ]

Today I'm thankful for:

1 [   ]

2 [   ]

3 [   ]

How I feel today:

HAPPY   EXCITED   TIRED   SAD
○   ○   ○   ○

SURPRISED   MAD   LONELY   SILLY
○   ○   ○   ○

Something wonderful will happen tomorrow:

1 _____

2 _____

3 _____

Date _____

Today I'm thankful for:

1 _____

2 _____

3 _____

How I feel today:

HAPPY   EXCITED   TIRED   SAD

◯   ◯   ◯   ◯

SURPRISED   MAD   LONELY   SILLY

◯   ◯   ◯   ◯

Something wonderful will happen tomorrow:

1 _____

2 _____

3 _____

Date [ ]

Today I'm thankful for:

1 [ ]

2 [ ]

3 [ ]

How I feel today:

HAPPY   EXCITED   TIRED   SAD
◯   ◯   ◯   ◯

SURPRISED   MAD   LONELY   SILLY
◯   ◯   ◯   ◯

Something wonderful will happen tomorrow:

1 _____

2 _____

3 _____

Date [ ]

Today I'm thankful for:

1 [ ]

2 [ ]

3 [ ]

How I feel today:

HAPPY	EXCITED	TIRED	SAD
◯	◯	◯	◯

SURPRISED	MAD	LONELY	SILLY
◯	◯	◯	◯

Something wonderful will happen tomorrow:

1 _____

2 _____

3 _____

The best things that happened to me

_____

_____

_____

_____

People I'm thankful for

_____

_____

_____

_____

I learned

_____

_____

_____

_____

Date [   ]

Today I'm thankful for:

1 [   ]

2 [   ]

3 [   ]

How I feel today:

HAPPY   EXCITED   TIRED   SAD
○   ○   ○   ○

SURPRISED   MAD   LONELY   SILLY
○   ○   ○   ○

Something wonderful will happen tomorrow:

1 _____

2 _____

3 _____

Date [   ]

Today I'm thankful for:

1 [   ]

2 [   ]

3 [   ]

How I feel today:

HAPPY   EXCITED   TIRED   SAD
( )   ( )   ( )   ( )

SURPRISED   MAD   LONELY   SILLY
( )   ( )   ( )   ( )

Something wonderful will happen tomorrow:

1 _____

2 _____

3 _____

Date [   ]

Today I'm thankful for:

1 [   ]

2 [   ]

3 [   ]

How I feel today:

HAPPY	EXCITED	TIRED	SAD
◯	◯	◯	◯

SURPRISED	MAD	LONELY	SILLY
◯	◯	◯	◯

Something wonderful will happen tomorrow:

1 _____

2 _____

3 _____

Date [   ]

Today I'm thankful for:

1 [   ]

2 [   ]

3 [   ]

How I feel today:

HAPPY   EXCITED   TIRED   SAD
◯   ◯   ◯   ◯

SURPRISED   MAD   LONELY   SILLY
◯   ◯   ◯   ◯

Something wonderful will happen tomorrow:

1 _____

2 _____

3 _____

Date [   ]

Today I'm thankful for:

1 [   ]

2 [   ]

3 [   ]

How I feel today:

HAPPY   EXCITED   TIRED   SAD
( )   ( )   ( )   ( )

SURPRISED   MAD   LONELY   SILLY
( )   ( )   ( )   ( )

Something wonderful will happen tomorrow:

1 _____

2 _____

3 _____

Date [   ]

Today I'm thankful for:

1 [   ]

2 [   ]

3 [   ]

How I feel today:

HAPPY	EXCITED	TIRED	SAD
◯	◯	◯	◯

SURPRISED	MAD	LONELY	SILLY
◯	◯	◯	◯

Something wonderful will happen tomorrow:

1 _____

2 _____

3 _____

Date

Today I'm thankful for:

1
2
3

How I feel today:

HAPPY   EXCITED   TIRED   SAD

○   ○   ○   ○

SURPRISED   MAD   LONELY   SILLY

○   ○   ○   ○

Something wonderful will happen tomorrow:

1 _____

2 _____

3 _____

Follow your dreams

I have a dream _____

_____

_____

_____

I have a dream _____

_____

_____

_____

I have a dream _____

_____

_____

_____

Date [   ]

Today I'm thankful for:

1 [   ]

2 [   ]

3 [   ]

How I feel today:

HAPPY   EXCITED   TIRED   SAD
( )   ( )   ( )   ( )

SURPRISED   MAD   LONELY   SILLY
( )   ( )   ( )   ( )

Something wonderful will happen tomorrow:

1 _____

2 _____

3 _____

Date _____

Today I'm thankful for:

1 _____

2 _____

3 _____

How I feel today:

HAPPY   EXCITED   TIRED   SAD
○   ○   ○   ○

SURPRISED   MAD   LONELY   SILLY
○   ○   ○   ○

Something wonderful will happen tomorrow:

1 _____

2 _____

3 _____

Date

Today I'm thankful for:

1

2

3

How I feel today:

HAPPY   EXCITED   TIRED   SAD

◯   ◯   ◯   ◯

SURPRISED   MAD   LONELY   SILLY

◯   ◯   ◯   ◯

Something wonderful will happen tomorrow:

1 _____

2 _____

3 _____

Date [   ]

Today I'm thankful for:

1 [   ]

2 [   ]

3 [   ]

How I feel today:

HAPPY   EXCITED   TIRED   SAD

◯   ◯   ◯   ◯

SURPRISED   MAD   LONELY   SILLY

◯   ◯   ◯   ◯

Something wonderful will happen tomorrow:

1 _____

2 _____

3 _____

Date [   ]

Today I'm thankful for:

1 [   ]

2 [   ]

3 [   ]

How I feel today:

HAPPY   EXCITED   TIRED   SAD

◯   ◯   ◯   ◯

SURPRISED   MAD   LONELY   SILLY

◯   ◯   ◯   ◯

Something wonderful will happen tomorrow:

1 _____

2 _____

3 _____

Date [＿＿＿＿＿]

Today I'm thankful for:

1 [＿＿＿＿＿＿＿＿＿＿＿＿＿＿]
2 [＿＿＿＿＿＿＿＿＿＿＿＿＿＿]
3 [＿＿＿＿＿＿＿＿＿＿＿＿＿＿]

How I feel today:

HAPPY ◯   EXCITED ◯   TIRED ◯   SAD ◯

SURPRISED ◯   MAD ◯   LONELY ◯   SILLY ◯

Something wonderful will happen tomorrow:

1 ＿＿＿＿＿＿＿＿＿＿＿＿＿＿＿＿＿＿＿

2 ＿＿＿＿＿＿＿＿＿＿＿＿＿＿＿＿＿＿＿

3 ＿＿＿＿＿＿＿＿＿＿＿＿＿＿＿＿＿＿＿

Date [   ]

Today I'm thankful for:

1 [   ]

2 [   ]

3 [   ]

How I feel today:

HAPPY ◯   EXCITED ◯   TIRED ◯   SAD ◯

SURPRISED ◯   MAD ◯   LONELY ◯   SILLY ◯

Something wonderful will happen tomorrow:

1 _____

2 _____

3 _____

DRAW YOUR DREAM

If you can dream it, You can do it!
- Walt Disney

Date

Today I'm thankful for:

1
2
3

How I feel today:

HAPPY   EXCITED   TIRED   SAD

◯   ◯   ◯   ◯

SURPRISED   MAD   LONELY   SILLY

◯   ◯   ◯   ◯

Something wonderful will happen tomorrow:

1 _____

2 _____

3 _____

Date [   ]

Today I'm thankful for:

1 [   ]

2 [   ]

3 [   ]

How I feel today:

HAPPY   EXCITED   TIRED   SAD
( )   ( )   ( )   ( )

SURPRISED   MAD   LONELY   SILLY
( )   ( )   ( )   ( )

Something wonderful will happen tomorrow:

1 _____

2 _____

3 _____

Date

Today I'm thankful for:

1

2

3

How I feel today:

HAPPY　　　EXCITED　　　TIRED　　　SAD

○　　　　　○　　　　　○　　　　　○

SURPRISED　　MAD　　　LONELY　　SILLY

○　　　　　○　　　　　○　　　　　○

Something wonderful will happen tomorrow:

1 _____

2 _____

3 _____

Date

Today I'm thankful for:

1
2
3

How I feel today:

HAPPY   EXCITED   TIRED   SAD

○   ○   ○   ○

SURPRISED   MAD   LONELY   SILLY

○   ○   ○   ○

Something wonderful will happen tomorrow:

1 _____

2 _____

3 _____

Date [_____]

Today I'm thankful for:

1 [_____]

2 [_____]

3 [_____]

How I feel today:

HAPPY   EXCITED   TIRED   SAD

◯   ◯   ◯   ◯

SURPRISED   MAD   LONELY   SILLY

◯   ◯   ◯   ◯

Something wonderful will happen tomorrow:

1 _____

2 _____

3 _____

Date [   ]

Today I'm thankful for:

1 [   ]

2 [   ]

3 [   ]

How I feel today:

HAPPY	EXCITED	TIRED	SAD
◯	◯	◯	◯
SURPRISED	MAD	LONELY	SILLY
◯	◯	◯	◯

Something wonderful will happen tomorrow:

1 _____

2 _____

3 _____

Date

Today I'm thankful for:

1

2

3

How I feel today:

HAPPY   EXCITED   TIRED   SAD

◯   ◯   ◯   ◯

SURPRISED   MAD   LONELY   SILLY

◯   ◯   ◯   ◯

Something wonderful will happen tomorrow:

1 _____

2 _____

3 _____

The best things that happened to me

_____

_____

_____

_____

People I'm thankful for

_____

_____

_____

I learned

_____

_____

_____

_____

Date

Today I'm thankful for:

1

2

3

How I feel today:

HAPPY   EXCITED   TIRED   SAD

○   ○   ○   ○

SURPRISED   MAD   LONELY   SILLY

○   ○   ○   ○

Something wonderful will happen tomorrow:

1 _____

2 _____

3 _____

Date [   ]

Today I'm thankful for:

1 [   ]

2 [   ]

3 [   ]

How I feel today:

HAPPY   EXCITED   TIRED   SAD
( )   ( )   ( )   ( )

SURPRISED   MAD   LONELY   SILLY
( )   ( )   ( )   ( )

Something wonderful will happen tomorrow:

1 _____

2 _____

3 _____

Date

Today I'm thankful for:

1
2
3

How I feel today:

HAPPY	EXCITED	TIRED	SAD
◯	◯	◯	◯

SURPRISED	MAD	LONELY	SILLY
◯	◯	◯	◯

Something wonderful will happen tomorrow:

1 _____

2 _____

3 _____

Date [   ]

Today I'm thankful for:

1 [   ]

2 [   ]

3 [   ]

How I feel today:

HAPPY   EXCITED   TIRED   SAD

◯   ◯   ◯   ◯

SURPRISED   MAD   LONELY   SILLY

◯   ◯   ◯   ◯

Something wonderful will happen tomorrow:

1 _____

2 _____

3 _____

Date [_____]

Today I'm thankful for:

1 [_____]

2 [_____]

3 [_____]

How I feel today:

HAPPY	EXCITED	TIRED	SAD
◯	◯	◯	◯

SURPRISED	MAD	LONELY	SILLY
◯	◯	◯	◯

Something wonderful will happen tomorrow:

1 _____

2 _____

3 _____

Date [   ]

Today I'm thankful for:

1 [   ]

2 [   ]

3 [   ]

How I feel today:

HAPPY   EXCITED   TIRED   SAD
◯   ◯   ◯   ◯

SURPRISED   MAD   LONELY   SILLY
◯   ◯   ◯   ◯

Something wonderful will happen tomorrow:

1 _____

2 _____

3 _____

Date [   ]

Today I'm thankful for:

1 [   ]

2 [   ]

3 [   ]

How I feel today:

HAPPY   EXCITED   TIRED   SAD

◯   ◯   ◯   ◯

SURPRISED   MAD   LONELY   SILLY

◯   ◯   ◯   ◯

Something wonderful will happen tomorrow:

1 _____

2 _____

3 _____

Follow your dreams

I have a dream _____

_____

_____

_____

I have a dream _____

_____

_____

_____

I have a dream _____

_____

_____

_____

Date [ ]

Today I'm thankful for:

1 [ ]

2 [ ]

3 [ ]

How I feel today:

HAPPY   EXCITED   TIRED   SAD

◯   ◯   ◯   ◯

SURPRISED   MAD   LONELY   SILLY

◯   ◯   ◯   ◯

Something wonderful will happen tomorrow:

1 _____

2 _____

3 _____

Date [   ]

Today I'm thankful for:

1 [   ]

2 [   ]

3 [   ]

How I feel today:

HAPPY	EXCITED	TIRED	SAD
◯	◯	◯	◯

SURPRISED	MAD	LONELY	SILLY
◯	◯	◯	◯

Something wonderful will happen tomorrow:

1 _____

2 _____

3 _____

Date

Today I'm thankful for:

1
2
3

How I feel today:

HAPPY   EXCITED   TIRED   SAD

◯   ◯   ◯   ◯

SURPRISED   MAD   LONELY   SILLY

◯   ◯   ◯   ◯

Something wonderful will happen tomorrow:

1 _____

2 _____

3 _____

Date _____

Today I'm thankful for:

1 _____

2 _____

3 _____

How I feel today:

HAPPY ◯   EXCITED ◯   TIRED ◯   SAD ◯

SURPRISED ◯   MAD ◯   LONELY ◯   SILLY ◯

Something wonderful will happen tomorrow:

1 _____

2 _____

3 _____

Date [   ]

Today I'm thankful for:

1 [   ]

2 [   ]

3 [   ]

How I feel today:

HAPPY   EXCITED   TIRED   SAD
◯   ◯   ◯   ◯

SURPRISED   MAD   LONELY   SILLY
◯   ◯   ◯   ◯

Something wonderful will happen tomorrow:

1 _____

2 _____

3 _____

Date

Today I'm thankful for:

1.
2.
3.

How I feel today:

HAPPY   EXCITED   TIRED   SAD

◯   ◯   ◯   ◯

SURPRISED   MAD   LONELY   SILLY

◯   ◯   ◯   ◯

Something wonderful will happen tomorrow:

1 _____

2 _____

3 _____

Date [   ]

Today I'm thankful for:

1 [   ]

2 [   ]

3 [   ]

How I feel today:

HAPPY	EXCITED	TIRED	SAD
◯	◯	◯	◯

SURPRISED	MAD	LONELY	SILLY
◯	◯	◯	◯

Something wonderful will happen tomorrow:

1 _____

2 _____

3 _____

DRAW YOUR DREAM

If you can dream it, You can do it!
- Walt Disney

Date

Today I'm thankful for:

1
2
3

How I feel today:

HAPPY   EXCITED   TIRED   SAD
○   ○   ○   ○

SURPRISED   MAD   LONELY   SILLY
○   ○   ○   ○

Something wonderful will happen tomorrow:

1 _____

2 _____

3 _____

Date _____

Today I'm thankful for:

1 _____

2 _____

3 _____

How I feel today:

HAPPY   EXCITED   TIRED   SAD

◯   ◯   ◯   ◯

SURPRISED   MAD   LONELY   SILLY

◯   ◯   ◯   ◯

Something wonderful will happen tomorrow:

1 _____

2 _____

3 _____

Date _____

Today I'm thankful for:

1 _____

2 _____

3 _____

How I feel today:

HAPPY ⭕   EXCITED ⭕   TIRED ⭕   SAD ⭕

SURPRISED ⭕   MAD ⭕   LONELY ⭕   SILLY ⭕

Something wonderful will happen tomorrow:

1 _____

2 _____

3 _____

Date [   ]

Today I'm thankful for:

1 [   ]

2 [   ]

3 [   ]

How I feel today:

HAPPY ○   EXCITED ○   TIRED ○   SAD ○

SURPRISED ○   MAD ○   LONELY ○   SILLY ○

Something wonderful will happen tomorrow:

1 _____

2 _____

3 _____

Date

Today I'm thankful for:

1
2
3

How I feel today:

HAPPY   EXCITED   TIRED   SAD

◯   ◯   ◯   ◯

SURPRISED   MAD   LONELY   SILLY

◯   ◯   ◯   ◯

Something wonderful will happen tomorrow:

1 _____

2 _____

3 _____

Date [＿＿＿＿＿＿]

Today I'm thankful for:

1 [＿＿＿＿＿＿＿＿＿＿＿＿＿＿＿＿]

2 [＿＿＿＿＿＿＿＿＿＿＿＿＿＿＿＿]

3 [＿＿＿＿＿＿＿＿＿＿＿＿＿＿＿＿]

How I feel today:

HAPPY	EXCITED	TIRED	SAD
○	○	○	○

SURPRISED	MAD	LONELY	SILLY
○	○	○	○

Something wonderful will happen tomorrow:

1 ＿＿＿＿＿＿＿＿＿＿＿＿＿＿＿＿＿＿＿

2 ＿＿＿＿＿＿＿＿＿＿＿＿＿＿＿＿＿＿＿

3 ＿＿＿＿＿＿＿＿＿＿＿＿＿＿＿＿＿＿＿

Date [ ]

Today I'm thankful for:

1 [ ]

2 [ ]

3 [ ]

How I feel today:

HAPPY ◯   EXCITED ◯   TIRED ◯   SAD ◯

SURPRISED ◯   MAD ◯   LONELY ◯   SILLY ◯

Something wonderful will happen tomorrow:

1 _____

2 _____

3 _____

The best things that happened to me

_____

_____

_____

_____

People I'm thankful for

_____

_____

_____

I learned

_____

_____

_____

_____

Date

Today I'm thankful for:

1

2

3

How I feel today:

HAPPY	EXCITED	TIRED	SAD
◯	◯	◯	◯
SURPRISED	MAD	LONELY	SILLY
◯	◯	◯	◯

Something wonderful will happen tomorrow:

1 _____

2 _____

3 _____

Date [ ]

Today I'm thankful for:

1 [ ]

2 [ ]

3 [ ]

How I feel today:

HAPPY ◯   EXCITED ◯   TIRED ◯   SAD ◯

SURPRISED ◯   MAD ◯   LONELY ◯   SILLY ◯

Something wonderful will happen tomorrow:

1 _____

2 _____

3 _____

Date [　　　　　　　　]

Today I'm thankful for:

1 [　　　　　　　　　　　　　　　　　]

2 [　　　　　　　　　　　　　　　　　]

3 [　　　　　　　　　　　　　　　　　]

How I feel today:

HAPPY　　○　　EXCITED　　○　　TIRED　　○　　SAD　　○

SURPRISED　　○　　MAD　　○　　LONELY　　○　　SILLY　　○

Something wonderful will happen tomorrow:

1 _____

2 _____

3 _____

Date [   ]

Today I'm thankful for:

1 [   ]

2 [   ]

3 [   ]

How I feel today:

HAPPY   EXCITED   TIRED   SAD
○   ○   ○   ○

SURPRISED   MAD   LONELY   SILLY
○   ○   ○   ○

Something wonderful will happen tomorrow:

1 _____

2 _____

3 _____

Date

Today I'm thankful for:

1
2
3

How I feel today:

| HAPPY | EXCITED | TIRED | SAD |
| ○ | ○ | ○ | ○ |

| SURPRISED | MAD | LONELY | SILLY |
| ○ | ○ | ○ | ○ |

Something wonderful will happen tomorrow:

1 _____

2 _____

3 _____

Date [ ]

Today I'm thankful for:

1 [ ]

2 [ ]

3 [ ]

How I feel today:

HAPPY	EXCITED	TIRED	SAD
◯	◯	◯	◯

SURPRISED	MAD	LONELY	SILLY
◯	◯	◯	◯

Something wonderful will happen tomorrow:

1 _____

2 _____

3 _____

Date [ ]

Today I'm thankful for:

1 [ ]

2 [ ]

3 [ ]

How I feel today:

HAPPY   EXCITED   TIRED   SAD
◯   ◯   ◯   ◯

SURPRISED   MAD   LONELY   SILLY
◯   ◯   ◯   ◯

Something wonderful will happen tomorrow:

1 _____

2 _____

3 _____

Follow your dreams

I have a dream _____
_____
_____
_____

I have a dream _____
_____
_____
_____

I have a dream _____
_____
_____
_____

Date [   ]

Today I'm thankful for:

1 [   ]

2 [   ]

3 [   ]

How I feel today:

HAPPY   EXCITED   TIRED   SAD
○   ○   ○   ○

SURPRISED   MAD   LONELY   SILLY
○   ○   ○   ○

Something wonderful will happen tomorrow:

1 _____

2 _____

3 _____

Date [　　　　　　]

Today I'm thankful for:

1 [　　　　　　　　　　　　　　　　　　]

2 [　　　　　　　　　　　　　　　　　　]

3 [　　　　　　　　　　　　　　　　　　]

How I feel today:

HAPPY	EXCITED	TIRED	SAD
◯	◯	◯	◯

SURPRISED	MAD	LONELY	SILLY
◯	◯	◯	◯

Something wonderful will happen tomorrow:

1 _____

2 _____

3 _____

Date [   ]

Today I'm thankful for:

1 [   ]

2 [   ]

3 [   ]

How I feel today:

HAPPY   EXCITED   TIRED   SAD
( )   ( )   ( )   ( )

SURPRISED   MAD   LONELY   SILLY
( )   ( )   ( )   ( )

Something wonderful will happen tomorrow:

1 _____

2 _____

3 _____

Date

Today I'm thankful for:

1

2

3

How I feel today:

HAPPY   EXCITED   TIRED   SAD

◯   ◯   ◯   ◯

SURPRISED   MAD   LONELY   SILLY

◯   ◯   ◯   ◯

Something wonderful will happen tomorrow:

1 _____

2 _____

3 _____

Date [   ]

Today I'm thankful for:

1 [   ]

2 [   ]

3 [   ]

How I feel today:

HAPPY   EXCITED   TIRED   SAD
( )   ( )   ( )   ( )

SURPRISED   MAD   LONELY   SILLY
( )   ( )   ( )   ( )

Something wonderful will happen tomorrow:

1 _____

2 _____

3 _____

Date [   ]

Today I'm thankful for:

1 [   ]

2 [   ]

3 [   ]

How I feel today:

HAPPY   EXCITED   TIRED   SAD
( )   ( )   ( )   ( )

SURPRISED   MAD   LONELY   SILLY
( )   ( )   ( )   ( )

Something wonderful will happen tomorrow:

1 _____

2 _____

3 _____

Date ⬡

Today I'm thankful for:

1 ⬡

2 ⬡

3 ⬡

How I feel today:

HAPPY ○   EXCITED ○   TIRED ○   SAD ○

SURPRISED ○   MAD ○   LONELY ○   SILLY ○

Something wonderful will happen tomorrow:

1 _____

2 _____

3 _____

The best things that happened to me

_____

_____

_____

_____

People I'm thankful for

_____

_____

_____

_____

I learned

_____

_____

_____

_____

If your kids have enjoyed this book, please consider leaving a short review on the book Amazon page.
It will help others to make an informed decision before buying my book.

Regards,
Charlie Wright

Made in the USA
Coppell, TX
17 December 2019